COLOR WORKS

A System for Unorganized and Overwhelmed Teachers

COLOR WORKS

A System for Unorganized and Overwhelmed Teachers

Jana Pendleton

COLORWORKS © Copyright 2022 Jana Pendleton. All rights reserved.

No part of this publication may be reproduced, distributed, or transmitted in any form or by any means, including photocopying, recording, or other electronic or mechanical methods, without the prior written permission of the publisher, except in the case of brief quotations embodied in critical reviews and certain other noncommercial uses permitted by copyright law.

For more information, visit JanaPendleton.com.

979-8-88759-084-4 - paperback
979-8-88759-085-1 - ebook

Get Your Free Gift!

To get the best experience with this book,
I've found readers who download and use
my free participation sheets
are able to implement the
COLORWORKS System faster
and take the next steps needed to become
more organized using color!

You can find more by visiting:
www.janapendleton.com

I would like to dedicate this book to
my mom, Janice Meikle.
She taught me everything I know.

Contents

Foreword xi
Preface xiii
Introduction xv

PART 1: WHERE TO BEGIN 1

Chapter 1: Color-Coding Subjects 3
Chapter 2: Color-Coding Class Periods 12
Chapter 3: Attendance And Class Participation 17
Chapter 4: Other Essential Tips For Getting Started 25

PART 2: IN-DEPTH ORGANIZATION 35

Chapter 5: Teaching Materials 37
Chapter 6: Getting Students Organized 43
Chapter 7: Deep-Dive Organizing 49

PART 3: WHY THIS WORKS 65

Chapter 8: Student Buy-In 67
Chapter 9: Classroom Environment 69
Chapter 10: Advice And Lessons Learned 75
Suggested Resources 81
Acknowledgments 87
Author Bio 89

Foreword

Jana and I met at an FCS conference where we instantly became great friends. We could talk about anything: family, vacations, frustrations, class schedules, ideas we'd like to try, and how to cope with large class sizes and difficult student situations. You name it – we talked about it.

I was teaching so many different classes than I ever had before. I had a filing system that had worked fine in the past and even had many assignments organized online. Still, as every teacher knows, there are often piles of assignments waiting to be graded, filed, etc. and I was beside myself trying to be prepared to teach the next day and deal with the clutter that engulfed my life.

This is when I went to visit Jana at her school. Her classroom was in order, and she could find anything for any of her classes in her filing cabinets. There was a place for everything! I asked her how she became so organized, she just smiled and then we sat down with a cool beverage and her color story began.

Jana loves color and uses it to her advantage for organization. Color is easy to see and spot on the run. Her ideas about how to use different colored hanging file folders in filing cabinets to organize classes and units got me excited. She then came to my school; we looked at my space, and her magical mind went to work. She suggested areas where I could use different colors to announce information for each subject and class. She told me about using baskets to hold my class rolls, new assignments, and papers to return to students. She even helped me put my filing cabinets together! I already felt more excited about school to start than I had in years!

I began the school year using Jana's system and it worked! I had places to put things for each class, places to write schedules with matching baskets and clipboards that I could simply pick up to use each class period. I had places to file assignments, tests, and activities for each unit. I love opening my filing cabinets and finding exactly what I need because of color! It's saved me time, energy, and my sanity! Jana's ideas have put me back in order; I love this feeling and will use this system until I retire.

Jana's color system can work for any subject area, any class, and for any teacher. Whether you're a seasoned or newer teacher, you will benefit by using this system. Jana is intelligent, organized, full of ideas, kind, loving, and is also a great teacher. Together with her intellect and years of teaching experience, Jana has found a way to help many teachers along the path of becoming the teachers we all hope to be. Now that all of her great information is in this book, Jana's COLORWORKS system will be able to help so many more!

—Lois Nielsen, colleague and Level 2 Professional Educator

Preface

We teach to make a difference. There is nothing better than to see the lightbulb moment when a student really gets it or when the student who used to skip class all the time is now showing up every day and engaged in your class. We teach because we love the kids. We teach because we love our subject matter. We teach because we're good at what we do.

What we don't count on is the difference teaching will make in our lives outside of school. It seems to take over, or at least trickle its way in, no matter what. Our days feel like they last forever, and the work is never ending. It follows us home, and even when it doesn't, it always takes up space in our brain. The piles of paperwork to grade, to file, to report to someone else, or to turn into our "next great teaching moment" tend to envelop our lives. No big deal, we'll get to it later. We pack it up in our backpack and take it home, only to carry it back to school untouched the next morning. The alternative is that we do the work on our free time and miss something else important to us, or to someone we love.

What if you had an easy-to-set-up workable system for filing paperwork, grading, planning, and storing resources? What if you didn't have to think about what you needed for each class period, didn't have to think about where things belong, or where to locate something you might need? What if you saw a pile of folders full of paper and knew exactly where to file them without hesitation? That is what this book is about.

Over the last twenty-plus years of teaching, I have developed a system using color-coding and some of my very favorite tools to make my work life so much easier. I teach high school, which means I have six class periods over two days with different subjects nearly every period. I could never do it all without using this method. In this book, I will show you step-by-step how to implement my system into one that will work the best for you and your classroom. It has taken me decades to build this, and you will benefit from that by having it all laid out for you, right here, from the ground up!

Introduction

As a kid, I just thought everybody had a color. One color that was just theirs alone . . . the color of their water cup, their towel, the plastic hangers in their closet, the four allotted wooden hangers in the coat closet, and possibly even their underwear. I was told that if I wanted a drink, I was supposed to use the same water cup over and over again until after dinner when it went into the dishwasher. If there were wet towels left on the bathroom floor and no one would own up to them, the colors of the towels gave away the culprits.

My color was pink, my sister's was yellow, and our two brothers' were blue and green. In the family coat closet, each of us had four wooden hangers. The nice ones, like in stores. Our names were written on masking tape attached to each hanger with big, fat yarn in our specific color tied on the hook in a bow. We didn't, in any way, each have four coats of our own. The extra one or two hangers were for our friends' coats. Underneath each of our sets of hangers was a cardboard box with our hat, mittens, and boots. Today those boxes would be clear plastic bins or cute woven bamboo baskets labeled with our color by tape or ribbon. The newly available plastic hangers in our closets were our same colors as well.

But as far as I know, mine was the only color-coded underwear. From what I remember my mom telling me, it was easy to pull out all the red (i.e., a shade of pink) panties from the dryer and put them away without having to sort through them all. With originally nine kids living at home, is there any wonder why my mom came up with these ideas?

I have carried on the color traditions with my own children. When their friends visit, they are also assigned a specific cup to drink out of. Better remember whose is whose or suffer the consequences. I did not want to wash potentially a dozen-plus glasses every day. Today, even my grandchildren pick a favorite cup when they come to visit. I don't have to ask which one they want anymore—even though I never actually assigned them a color to begin with—they always choose the same ones.

I don't mean to say color took a detour out of my life once I left home. I have always found myself looking at colorful items first, always loved the colors pink and purple, and hardly ever owned anything neutral. It has helped that I *really* am my mother's daughter. How could I not be? Mom loved colorful things, and purple was her favorite color too! Her kitchen cupboards were hot pink, and the grout in her kitchen tile was purple! She had the most organized closets, drawers, and cupboards I'd ever seen, rivaling those in books and magazines. They looked like they were straight out of a store! Even her garage looked perfect!

When I went back to college to become a teacher, my Intro to Teaching class went on a field trip out of state. One of the featured speakers created curriculum for her state office. She worked from home, so we all piled into her living room. There were boxes, binders, and posters for every class subject. She had color-coded everything according to its field of study.

This one visit changed my life. It didn't just speak to me, it spoke to my soul! I was so impressed that I can still, to this day, remember sitting in her living room taking it all in, vowing to put everything I already knew by heart into practice. I was envious sitting there. I couldn't wait until I had my own classroom to organize by color! I knew I'd be good at it, I just didn't know when I would need it . . . exactly.

Later, in a family finance class, I was assigned to create a personal filing system for important papers. I hadn't forgotten that field trip experience from a couple of years earlier. It was time to put my inherent knowledge to work!

My personal files were blue, money management files were yellow, credit was orange, investments were green, medical files were pink, housing was gray, insurance was lavender, and taxes were, of course, red. Since I only needed a couple files of each color, I purchased really colorful folders, and it was beautiful! My professor even commented as such! Incidentally, I still use the same filing system at home today—including the same colors representing the same topic areas. With all things digital, the only difference is I don't file every piece of paper like I used to.

All of this is leading into how color-coding has been and *always will be* an integral part of my life, even before I knew what to call it. Having been raised this way was normal to me. I love to go into stores where the merchandise has just been reorganized. Seeing everything all lined up by color makes me feel warm and fuzzy inside. When I'm somewhere there are small items, such as in the makeup aisle or in the office supply areas, I find myself straightening up after the thoughtless toss of long-before shoppers. Little did I know my crazy quirkiness would practically save my life, so-to-speak, in the future.

Twenty years ago, I was at the top of my game. I had been accepted into not just one but two PhD programs: one at Brigham Young University and the other at Utah State University. I had just completed my master's degree in Marriage, Family, and Human Development at BYU with a culminating thesis of 123 pages. My mind was on fire, well at least for me. I was engaged to marry my sweetheart, and we were planning to join our two kids each into a newly blended family.

My husband and I chose to bond our two families by adding an additional child to the mix. After enduring an amazing, yet severe, sudden-onset, pre-eclamptic, and traumatic premature birth experience (saving the telling of that story for another day), I found myself with a huge loss of short-term memory and thought-processing ability that I had previously enjoyed. I quickly realized this when I couldn't remember having fed my baby or how long ago I'd changed his diaper. I wasn't sure when we had slept or for how long. I even had to get out a notebook and keep track of every single move in order to know what needed to be done the next time he cried. I began to doubt myself and felt confused all the time. I really thought I'd gain confidence by working through it day after day, like I had with my two older babies, but I didn't. Not by a long shot.

By that point, I was in the middle of my PhD and found myself struggling in my classes to lead a discussion on just a one-page article summary I'd written the night before. Luckily, I had some compassionate professors who were aware of the situation, and as soon as they gave me a small nudge toward what I was discussing, I picked right up where I'd left off. I could feel myself losing it, feeling confused, and forgetting even the most simple things I'd been doing every single day of my life.

The only way I could handle my crazy busy life was to come up with a set of routines and coping mechanisms. Even getting ready each morning became a mini nightmare for me. If I wavered from the specific order I'd set up for even the most mundane of tasks, I *always* forgot something. I'd forget to brush my teeth, to put on mascara, or even to put on a bra at one point. So I always went back to the routines of it all . . . and it saved me. It saved us.

This is when color-coding re-entered my everyday life. Using color makes it so I don't have to think or remember, so I can do what I had lost the ability to do. It began little by little. If I could print something out onto a brightly colored piece of paper rather than plain white, I could not only find it, I could somehow remember what it was about! Those one-page article summaries of mine became well known to my classmates. They were always copied onto fun colors, which quickly gave away who was in charge of our discussion that day. It somehow made them more fun, easier to read and discuss.

My textbooks looked like a work of art. Different colors of highlighters and ink pens had different meanings to me. Sometimes it reflected a level of importance in the text itself, and other days it was just what made me happy. But in the end, that's what brought me back to life. I began to feel like I could actually do this thing!

In the circles where I teach school, as well as those state-wide where I've presented workshops at professional conferences, I've come to be known for how much I love color . . . and how much I like things to be a certain way. I'm really not a fanatic, I can handle it when others don't agree or when they want to do things differently than I do. Really! However, for every naysayer, there are two others who think it is brilliant (even if it's just one small part of it), and that seems to make up the difference.

One new friend came up to me after a recent presentation and called me a "Rockstar!" Oh what a feeling! As I was telling this story to my husband, he said, "There's your first book topic right there!" I'd always wanted to write books but could never settle on just one topic, so . . . here we are. The rest is history as they say.

The best part of all is that each part of this system can work independently and can also be a good place to begin . . . even a good place to linger for a while. Mull it over in your mind, and as it begins to become second nature to you, then you can move to the next chapter if it feels right.

It has taken me years to get this far and to become immersed in it all. Start slow and small, give or take my ideas, but please just keep reading; bookmark areas you're interested in and try one tiny bit. Stop there if it is all you can make yourself do. If only one person gains an ounce of freedom by using my system, this book will have done its job. But what if there's more? It simply can't hurt to take a chance. What have you got to lose?

PART 1

Where To Begin

As much as we might love our job, there is definitely a downside to teaching: the difference it makes in our lives outside of school. Much of this involves paperwork, preparation, obtaining resources, planning, and working in the evening hours. Summer breaks are just a myth, at least for some of us.

In this section, I would like to introduce you to something that I believe can help. COLORWORKS is a system I have developed over decades—one step at a time. I finally feel like it is in a place where it can truly make a difference in other teacher's lives. It is not perfect for everyone as a whole, but there are so many different ideas included that I really feel could assist everyone in making small changes that will add up over time.

I've taught a university-level Methods of Teaching class to future teachers. I've mentored several student teachers as well as presented at state-level teacher conferences. Many of the new and veteran teachers attending each of those conferences have expressed interest in my ideas, so I've decided to put it all in one easily accessible place. I find that new teachers, especially during that difficult first year, become overwhelmed quickly. I also know that most first-year teachers are looking for inexpensive solutions for their needs. It comes down to time vs. money. Throughout our life we usually have, or value, one of these more than the other. Teachers are notorious for having to work on a budget, so this is how to get creative. I understand that there are nicer, more expensive options for some of the items I am about to introduce to you. But this is how I built the system from the beginning without having to invest a ton of money. This is the best thing I can do for these new teachers.

If you are able to go with a more expensive option for storing or organizing your items, then go for it. I've upgraded my system over the years as well. I've also written this out so you can start at any point that speaks to you. I highly suggest you begin reading through the book from the beginning, but if you find something that you want to complete right away, then do it! You can always go back and implement ideas from previous chapters. You'll be amazed how even one little change can make a huge difference.

CHAPTER 1

Color-Coding Subjects

I graduated from the University of Idaho with my bachelor's degree and teaching certificate in family and consumer sciences. This area of study is no longer just foods and sewing courses, but also includes interior design, fashion, personal finance, human development, and marriage and family classes. I began my first teaching job, luckily at my own high school, and was fortunate to work alongside some of the same great faculty who'd taught me. I was part-time and taught two class periods per day, two different subjects per trimester, or six classes per year.

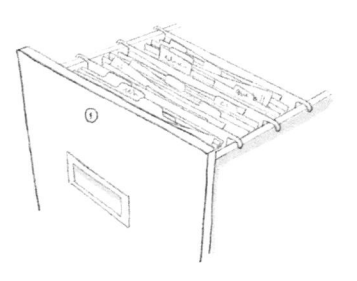

I'll never forget the first time I looked into a working teacher's filing cabinet full of white papers, manila file folders, and dark-green hanging file folders. I'm not saying there's anything necessarily wrong with it, but I knew it looked exactly like every other drawer in the cabinet. All of the file tabs were written in smudged pencil (I assume so the files could be recycled and used again), and every one of them looked exactly the same. If I wanted to find anything specific, I was going to have to try reading every single file tab until I found the particular one I was looking for. It was just so overwhelming (and a bit boring). But more importantly, it just wasn't me.

I have to admit, my own teaching file drawers looked almost exactly the same way in the beginning, minus the smudgy pencil of course! My school provided the usual manila folders and dark-green hanging file folders, so that was a win for me! However, if more than three of those file folders lay on my desk at a time, I found myself having to take the time to search out which one belonged in which drawer. Ultimately, I knew what needed to be done.

GETTING STARTED

I decided the solution would be to color-code my different subjects by using colored folders like those I had used in my personal filing system. However, I was young and poor; I knew I couldn't afford to buy all new colored folders for as many files as I needed. Instead, I went to the store and purchased my first two packages of file folder labels, each with a different colored stripe on top. One package of labels was blue for my sewing class and the other was yellow for Life Management. It was a good start, but I knew it was only the beginning. If, for some reason, you don't like to use labels on your file folders, you can just color the top of each file folder's tab with whichever color you choose for that subject using a marker.

I clearly printed on each file's label with a dark black permanent marker so it was easy to read. If I wanted to reuse the folder for something else, I just covered the label with a new one and it was ready to go! Each hanging file folder would hold about five manila folders, and each of the folders were full of copies of handouts for the entire unit of study. The hanging folder was labeled with the unit's name such as Introduction, for example. Then within the hanging folder would be all the manila folders, each holding a worksheet, activity, review, or quiz for that unit. Sometimes there are more manila folders than will fit within one hanging folder, so there can be multiple hanging folders for one unit. The front one, however, is the only one labeled with the name of the unit on the clear plastic tab provided. The others are just placed behind that one.

Next, I clearly labeled each drawer of my filing cabinet with the matching color cardstock. Now when more than one folder lay on my desk, I only had to glance over at the file cabinet, and I knew exactly in which drawer it belonged. Merriam-Webster's Tenth Edition definition of color states that it is, in fact "a visual perception that enables one to differentiate otherwise identical objects."[1] Colors are so much more easily identifiable than reading the label on every single item. Easy peasy!

As a brand-new teacher, beginning this way can create an easy, fairly inexpensive system to start and keep up with. If creating new folders, just add the correctly colored label as you create each folder. This works well even if you only teach one subject. It doesn't matter what subject or grade you teach—whether it's elementary or secondary school, part-time or full-time—these ideas *will* work for you. Just adjust them to fit your situation.

You'll also have files that aren't necessarily used for teaching a class but that pertain to your career, your school, or your department. And you may need to be able to keep track of them easily. Examples of these files could be Testing, Licensure, Registrations, Conferences, Grades, etc. These files would be considered just one category such as Management and be given a color and drawer to keep them separate from your teaching files.

If you're a more seasoned teacher who is interested in putting *some* of this to use but thinks it might just be too much work to change everything over, I would suggest adding the colored label as you work your way through each of your files, each consecutive term, one file at a time. This will also be a great way to be able to look back and see which files you are actually using and which ones may need to be weeded out. Either way, I promise you'll thank me later!

---

[1] "Color," *Merriam-Webster's Collegiate Dictionary, 10th ed.* (Springfield, MA: Merriam Webster: 1998): 226.

Each subject gets its own file drawer—no matter what. Any files in the drawer used solely for reference, or those that are full of future ideas waiting to be implemented, need to "hang out" in the very back of the drawer. If they have extra copies in them, recycle those. You don't want these files taking up too much room, and you definitely don't want to intermix them together with the "working" files in the drawer.

Work your way from the front of the drawer toward the back. This may seem obvious to many, but there are others who may file things alphabetically or with some other unique method. I like it all ordered chronologically, as you use it, from the beginning of the semester until the end. I can usually fit a full semester course into just one file drawer—two if absolutely necessary. Currently I only have one subject that takes up two full drawers.

Eventually I realized that each different assignment, worksheet, or quiz needed more space due to the number of copies I would have to have ready ahead of time. For this reason, I eventually transitioned over to using one hanging folder for each different item in place of using separate manila folders for each. I just found that copies for an entire class, or two, would fit better that way.

For labeling purposes, I put the plastic tab labels in the same location on each hanging folder for the entire unit, such as in slots one to three on the far left. Then the tabs would be in slots four to six for those folders in the second unit, and then in slots seven to nine for the third unit, and finally use slots ten to twelve on the far right for the fourth unit. The fifth unit of study would start over again in the far left.

As time went on and I could afford it, I began to purchase hanging file folders in the course subject colors rather than just using the dark-green ones. Usually I was able to afford to change out one or two subjects per semester or year. Again, for simplicity's sake, I would just replace one folder at a time as I used it for class. It makes it easier to see which files I was actually using.

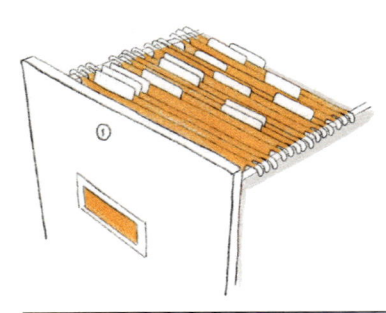

My advice would be to only purchase these colored hanging folders online as they are much less expensive and come in a greater variety of colors there as opposed to any office supply store around town. As a real-life example of how this can work, I am currently using red, pink, maroon, navy, yellow, purple, green, orange, blue, and teal for my subject files. Whew! That is a lot of different classes and filing drawers!

This system will obviously work well for any secondary teacher no matter the subject but can also work well for those who teach elementary. You don't even need to be a teacher to learn something new here that will work for you. With each new idea I introduce, just think of how it will equate to the paperwork and filing systems that you use in your everyday work or homelife situations.

CHOOSING COLORS

As a new term began, I would sometimes get lucky enough to reteach a subject, or I might have to begin teaching new subjects altogether. I had to then figure out which colors would represent any new subjects being taught. There really isn't a perfect method for doing this; I just used the colors that made sense to me. I remember an Advanced Foods class being green (think vegetables), Dating & Marriage was pink (think hearts), Fashion Strategies was a darker blue than the original sewing class had been because both subjects were clothing related.

If different courses are taught that have a common theme such as those just mentioned, or if they are in a sequential order such as Math 10A and Math 10B, try using different shades of the same color such as pink to red to maroon, or light blue to blue to navy. I know there are many teachers out there who teach less than six different subjects total. If this is the case, I would just use up to all six colors of the rainbow. I highly suggest you don't choose unusual colors (even if you love them) as you won't be able to find the supplies you'll need in those colors. If you stick with the six rainbow colors to start with, you can find just about every must-have tool I suggest you use in each of them. (See Suggested Resources for my must-haves list.)

I have taught over twelve different subjects in my career, but thankfully no more than seven in the same school year. In other words, I have had to get creative in assigning colors to subjects. Once a color system is in place, it becomes easier to remember and know what it represents at first glance. I honestly never have to think about where a file or box of items belongs.

It may sound somewhat complicated in the beginning, but it won't seem that way even a day or two later. If it happens to take up to a week or two to get used to it, don't give up. Don't over-complicate things. Any changes you make will be better than where you were when you started. Maybe just begin with one subject and one color; then when you feel ready, add a second color to a different subject, and then eventually a third one, and so on. Remember, you don't have to wait until a new term starts. Begin where you are today!

Often, there are files I don't necessarily want to get rid of but that I am not using at the moment; I just move those to the back of the drawer for a semester or two. After I repeat a subject the next semester, and if the file wasn't used a second time around, I usually empty it. Many times, I just make sure I have an electronic copy of the item, and then I will trash it. It's a simple method of de-junking your files.

If I were just starting out with this color system, I would get this far in color-coding my subjects, and use it for a while until it becomes easy. Chapter 5 is full of ideas on how to go deeper into the details of color-coding subjects. There are great ideas you can implement just one at a time. I purposefully put them in a separate chapter so it would not become overwhelming. Once you feel ready to dig in, go for it!

CHAPTER 2

Color-Coding Class Periods

All of these tips worked well for me, although I left that first teaching job after three-and-a-half years and ended up in graduate school. (Another story to save and tell at another time.) When I went back to teaching high school, I got a job where I was only going to be teaching one prep, or subject. It happened to be a year-long class, but I would be teaching it in six different class periods!

Now how was I going to keep that straight? I automatically decided my file system needed to be yellow as this class was similar to, and actually replacing, my class from the other high school. However, my previous color-coding arrangement for my teaching files couldn't keep six class periods of the same subject under control. Plus, now I'd had my baby and was having a more difficult time with my thought-processing abilities. What was I going to do?

One day in the midst of all of this adjustment, I happened to see one of those wire cube cubby organizers found in many college dorm rooms being used to store scrapbook paper. (If you Google "wire cube storage," you'll be able to find a bunch offered. They are available online from Amazon, Walmart, and Home Depot, just to name a few places. One of my friends also found them at Bed, Bath & Beyond recently.)

I remember being very impressed that it looked so professional while being so inexpensive at the same time. Rather than only using the five original sides meant to create a single open-front cube (top, bottom, two sides, and a back), there were several more squares zip-tied horizontally within the cube to create several slots (about twelve—each slot was around one inch tall) for different categories of paper. The result looked like it came straight out of the store itself.

Immediately, I saw how great that idea could be if I modified it a little bit to be used as new inboxes for my six class periods! I had previously just used wire or plastic baskets for assignments to be turned in. These baskets were stacked by twos and were provided by the school. I had never really liked them because they were small, filled up very quickly, and always tipped over. I had been keeping my eye out for anything that could work better, and I finally found it!

These cube organizers were fairly inexpensive so I purchased myself a box. I started by creating two cubes open on the front following the original plan specifications. I then added two more squares horizontally, evenly spaced within each cube, to create three shelf slots.

Two cubes zip-tied together made a total of six slots for papers to be turned in by students. I've used them stacked on top of each other or by having each cube sit side-by-side. It all depends upon where they will be located.

This was brilliant because it allowed for larger than regular 8.5" x 11" papers to fit into each slot. (I regularly assign projects that are odd sizes, and this system has worked perfectly for those—much, much better than the baskets from before.) I secured them tightly with clear zip ties and then wound colored pipe cleaners around the front of each slot in each of the six rainbow colors beginning with red and working towards purple. Six class periods, six colors. Ta-da!

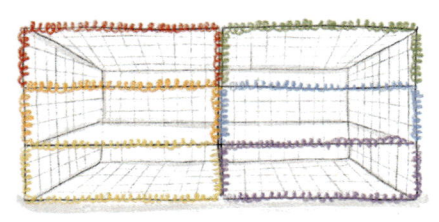

In the first cube, the top slot was red with orange below that in the center slot and then yellow woven into the bottom slot. The second cube had green on top, blue in the center, and purple on the bottom. I was going to be teaching three class periods on A day and three class periods on B day. It just happened to turn out that A day included the warm colors and B day included the cool colors. I swear it wasn't planned!

I find it important when using the six main colors that they are in their correct order. It is much easier for my brain to follow. To be completely honest, it doesn't make sense to me when the colors are mixed up and not used in the order of the rainbow; I would never know which class was going to be next without having to spend more time thinking about it. But to each their own. It's your system. Create one that makes sense to you!

This new inbox is how I came up with color-coding the different class periods *in addition to* having colors already assigned to my subjects. My first class on A day became the red class no matter if it was first period or second (with first period being my prep hour). Red was just the first class I taught during that day, followed by the second class of my day being orange, and last by the third class I taught being yellow. B day worked exactly the same way using green, blue, and then purple . . . no matter which period of the day was my prep hour.

Although this totally happened by accident, I will say that this is the single most important color-coding secret I use: *Class periods should have a color, even if your subjects don't.* So, if this speaks to you more than Chapter 1, start here first. It is important to note that the colors of your subjects *do not change.* They will stay the same no matter in which class period they are being taught. The files and drawers will stay the same colors you already gave them. The items being mentioned in this chapter will identify only the class period when they are being used.

The students follow this color-coding really well. They don't have to think which class period they're in either. They are just always the red class or the blue class for example. Many of them don't even notice that the subject matter has a color . . . only the class period. Have you ever noticed how often they come in and ask if it is A or B day?

At one point in my career, our school board wanted all high school teachers to teach seven class periods with only one prep hour every other day. Yes, it was going to be more work. No, I wouldn't have enough time to be ready for the next day. But the craziest thought running around in my head was what color was going to be class number seven? Ridiculous, I know. But it's the truth! That's how important this system has become in my life. Luckily it didn't come to pass.

A funny thing about using color is that even years later, when I see a particular student from the past, I may not remember their name, I may not even recognize them right away, but once I find out who they are, I can very often remember what color class period they were in! I swear it's true. I'll for sure not ever forget that the varsity quarterback who invited me to prom (jokingly) was in my green class. I remember saying it was pretty funny that I'd finally gotten asked out by the quarterback, just twenty years too late!

CHAPTER 3

Attendance And Class Participation

PARTICIPATION SHEETS

One reason why the students know exactly which color their class period is, is because they use my participation sheets. Some teachers will call these starter sheets. I have created a double-sided single page printed on cardstock in each of the six colors of the class periods I teach. One entire quarter fits on each side. This is how I take roll and keep track of attendance and participation points. I have usually copied them onto the bright bold colors, and at times they can be difficult to read. It also works well to use the tint of each of those colors such as pink, peach, canary, mint, baby blue, and lavender.

Each day the students pick these sheets up as they enter the classroom and write down the daily topic of the day, which is written on the board in the front. Then they should turn them right into the matching in-basket. On the board, I have sectioned off portions using colored electrical tape for each class period. I tell the students, "If you're writing on an orange piece of paper then write what is written in the orange box." I will say that I am amazed how many don't follow that instruction . . . especially if it is a finance class and they write down the word "birth" from Child Development! What are they thinking sometimes?

Having all students picking up their sheets off one table or desk can cause a bottleneck into the classroom. This is why, on the first day of the new semester when I hand out the original participation sheets, I have markers set out on their tables and have them fill in all of the dates for the entire quarter next to each day numbered 1–22. I have all of the dates written on the board for the current quarter. Make sure they only write on one side of the sheet or they tend to get things mixed up and put one random day's attendance on the back . . . this is how mistakes will happen. I just know this from having used them as long as I have. I will create attendance sheets for any absent students so they are available the next day of class.

Their name goes in easy-to-read handwriting with a *dark* marker on the top, and then I let them doodle or do graffiti around the perimeter of the page so their paper will look original to them. I tell them the more they write or draw, and the bolder it is, the better. Only rule is that it cannot be inside the table of information and it must be teacher appropriate. It makes picking them up at the beginning of class go so much faster, both from the table and also from the teacher if they are tardy (explained in the next paragraph). I've found that there are several students who just simply refuse to do this doodling. I don't understand why that is, but after a few weeks of trying to find their own paper, I'll usually put out the markers again for them to add to whatever they've previously done.

Right as the bell rings on every day thereafter, I pick up the rest of the pile of participation sheets that have not been previously picked up. It would make sense that these sheets belong to my tardy and absent students. In the beginning of the term, I have to remind them that if they haven't picked their paper up yet, I am going to start marking all the ones in my hand absent. I start to mark absences on the papers while I begin class, and if a student walks in late, I ask them to come pick theirs up from me. I will change the absence to a tardy (which they would prefer) and continue to teach. It would stand to reason that if students are added into the class later, they'll need to have new sheets made for them. Just make sure they begin on the same day number as the rest of the class rather than on day number one, which has already past.

These sheets make it so after the first or second day of class, I no longer have to take the time to read the roll. I enter attendance straight from the participation sheets in my hand after the bell has rung. I catch a lot of tardies this way. Also, it is very important that students only pick up their own paper even if they think their friend will be showing up. Remind them to turn them in as soon as class is beginning so they don't mix them in with their other papers and walk out the door with them. The sheets of all the present students get initialed or stamped in the attendance column. It's a great job for my TA! If a student is absent, make sure to fill in the topic of the day anyway, or draw a line through the topic area, to keep them writing the next daily topic on the correct line and date.

Yes, sometimes there are errors on either one or both of our parts, but the student soon won't forget to pick up their paper after their first mistaken absence (which of course I will fix). Another positive aspect of these sheets is that I can tell exactly what they missed by looking at their sheet and seeing the topic written for the particular day they were gone. If there is a substitute, I always have them write "sub" down for the daily topic. That helps explain away any errors in attendance or things they missed that I may not remember off the top of my head.

Another thing that I love about these sheets is the participation area. In the past, I have had codes for different infractions that I would write in this area, but now I just write down things like "no phones," "put your book away," "pay attention," etc. I much rather let them know I'm aware of what they were doing without making a big deal out of it in front of the class. It's also a good place to leave a note to the student like, "thanks for your great comments today" or "come see me about . . ."

This page also keeps track of their hall passes, of which I only allow two free ones per quarter for five minutes each. Any additional passes will cost them points. I do have a sign-out sheet where they are supposed to fill in the times they leave and return. I tend to be pretty lenient during the first week or so but then start to crack down on their number of passes. Finally, there is a column for the number of points being deducted for their behavior as well as for their unexcused absences and tardies or extra hall passes.

Because I am teaching high schoolers, I have a strong opinion when it comes to a student's behavior. On the first day I tell them that they are almost adults. If they want me to treat them as such, they should act like it. I will let them make choices which will have consequences if they abuse them—just like in real life. And it is written directly in my course disclosures and discussed on the first day of the semester.

The very best part of using these sheets is that the student sees what is written down *each day* when they write on them at the beginning of the next class period. This way *there are no surprises at midterm or end-of-term for points missed.* Hooray! They know every class period where they stand as far as participation points go. And if a parent complains, I just pull out the attendance sheet and show them what has been going on all term. One last thing, if you happen to use extra credit for getting students to volunteer, donate items to the class, not use any hall passes, etc., then this is a great place to keep track of all of that too!

Points are tallied and added to the gradebook at midterm and at the end-of-term. These points will count more in classes where we do a lot of work in-class and there needs to be more hands-on participation—rather than attending class and doing work that could be done at home. This may or may not work for you at your school or in your subject area, but since I teach CTE courses, some of them are much more labor intensive than others.

When a student comes to me at the end of the semester asking for extra credit or asking how they can raise their grade, I often ask them to first go find their participation sheet. I can see right away if the student has been in class and not abused privileges or if they have several unexcused absences or taken way too many hall passes and missed too much of class. I usually point that out to them and ask what they think I should do based on their prior behavior. It can become a great teaching moment sometimes.

PAPER BASKETS (I love these!)

If you still prefer to call roll and don't like the participation/attendance sheet idea, then here is my next best idea: colored paper baskets for each class period—color-coordinated of course! When first starting out, I found a set of these 14.25"W x 10"D x 3.25"H baskets at our local dollar store. They were all blue, and since I wanted them to be designated for each class period, I put the six colors of duct tape around the top of each basket and used them for a few years just like that.

Once I was able to afford to order my own set of correctly colored baskets, I purchased them from a higher-quality online store. (See Suggested Resources in back of book.) Now I use the old blue ones for other items and organizing supplies for myself.

I love having these class period-colored baskets for several reasons. Inside each I have a (dare I say color-coded) clipboard with a photo seating chart on it. It is printed on cardstock, laminated, and placed in a page protector so I can use it to take roll with a dry-erase marker if I am worried that students are taking advantage of the participation sheets.

I make the seating charts right at the beginning of the semester. I'll print out the student photos, cover each row of pictures with clear shipping tape as a sort of lamination. Just over the front is fine. My TA will cut out all of the photos and attach them to the clipboard with a pillow of masking or white artist tape. If you aren't sure what artist's tape is, it is similar to masking tape but thicker and whiter. It is also super sticky and easily removed—it's a must-have item in my book!

If I want to let the kids sit wherever they choose, I'll let them know that next time I'll be sending around a drawn-up seating chart to have them write their name on where they want to sit. Then I tell them that they can sit there until they "earn" the right to be moved. It takes a minute, but eventually they begin to understand my meaning. Otherwise, I usually do it the old-fashioned way . . . alphabetically by last name starting with table one. The clipboard always stays on top of items in the basket and helps me to learn my students' names and faces. Any graded papers needing to be returned to the students go in the bottom of the basket so I can easily remove the clipboard and pass the basket around to return those papers to their owners without taking precious time out of class.

While lesson planning, I will place any copies or files I might need for that class period in the top of the basket, along with any small items needed such as cards, dice, or a book. Any announcements or class-specific questions will go on sticky notes attached to the seating chart.

If something is left in my classroom after a class has just ended, I pick it up and place it in that class's basket and forget about it. Two days later when that class meets again, I say, "Oh yeah, this was left last time. Does it belong to anyone?" Very simple and yet so freeing at the same time. I really don't have to think or try to remember something over the weekend!

These baskets are just a super quick way to have a place to put items that I used to have to try to remember to hand out in class. If the office wants me to deliver something to a student or if another student asks me to, these really help. I've even used them as a way to help invite a student out to one of the school dances by another student!

CHAPTER 4

Other Essential Tips For Getting Started

PLANNING BOOKS

One very simple product that I have personally created is that of a really quite simple teacher planning book. At one conference I was told that it was their favorite part— "Just wait until she talks about it!" I previously had used the books provided by the school district for the first few years, and they worked all right I suppose. However, we all teach in different types of schools with different types of schedules and numbers of classes per day. I had to make mine fit my own situation.

There is one aspect that I feel should be universal, however, and that is that the days of the week should be written horizontally across the top of the page rather than vertically down the left side of the page. When looking at a calendar, *any* calendar, how are the days of the week formatted?

I have searched and searched for what's called a vertical-week planner and can only find a few here and there. This is why I decided to format my own school planner in which Monday through Friday go across the top of the page. Monday through Wednesday on the left side or back of a page, Thursday through the weekend on the right side or front of the page. This way when you open up the planner and lay it flat, the entire week is in order across the top of the book. These books are *very* basic and simple by design. I've found that I really don't use all of the extra bells and whistles that several planners provide. I want to see what's important to my day and that's it. The rest is in my phone calendar anyway.

We have four class periods per day on an A and B day schedule. Although I only teach three of the four class periods each day, my prep hour varies day-to-day and from semester-to-semester. I like to use the prep hour space to list any specific tasks I might need to finish during that time. Now here is where it gets interesting. Of course, I need to add color!

In the square set aside for my first class on A days, I draw a line with a red marker or other coloring method such as crayons or colored pencils vertically against the left side of the cell. Orange in the second class of the day and then yellow in the third class. Prep hours remain blank (second on A day and fifth on B day in illustration). On B days it proceeds in the same manner but with green, blue, and then purple. Go ahead and stop at this point until you feel more comfortable with using the planner. Then follow along with the next planner step.

Now I have to know which subject I am teaching in each of those class periods since I have so many different preparations. If it were just one subject such as in the past, I would skip over this second step. I use the color that represents the subject being taught during the red class period and draw a line horizontally across the top of the cell. (In the illustration this is the turquoise subject which is also taught in seventh and eighth periods on B days.) Then I do the same in each of the other five class periods I am teaching that term. Yes, it may look crazy at first, but as you go along, it will make perfect sense and you won't have to have written any of it down in words! That's the beauty of it all!

This book is a great place to add schedules including your own, your entire department's, the school's, and the district's calendar. I of course like to print all of this in color and add them just inside the front cover. The back of the book has lined pages from a legal pad for taking notes in meetings or reminders for next year, etc. I really do carry this book about everywhere!

In the circle you'll see I have sticky notes that fit just inside each of the squares. At the beginning of the term, I will put one (using the *subject's* color) in each of the squares where that subject is being taught. I'll write down topics on the sticky notes and place them in the order that I usually teach them. If something happens and I want to change the order, I'll just move the sticky notes around until I see that it works the way I would like. Once the date has passed, I will usually write it directly onto the page.

I'll add in vacations, birthdays, meetings, and professional development days. The days I am gone get a huge yellow X over the entire day so I can still read the plans for the day, but then I can easily see which days I've had a substitute over the school year. I spiral bind it all together, and for a fun cover, I laminate some cute paper or cardstock.

Many of you will notice that the participation sheet and two calendar pages are available for free download on a page in the front of this book. Just photocopy enough pages for every week of the school year. I like to use paper from sketch pads the best. It has a little texture and is heavier than regular paper but not quite as heavy as cardstock. Don't forget to add in the extra pages mentioned above as well as choose a fun cover for yourself. Check out my website janapendleton.com for information on any new products as they become available.

I really, really like the fact that I have books from all of my years of teaching. When I pick up a subject I last taught a few years ago, I just pull out that book and know exactly the order in which I would like the class to go. I do change things up a lot, but I've been known to keep notes on days when things went great, if I used a new idea and it bombed, or if I really like it just the way it is.

I know that this paper planning book works amazingly well for many but may not be your first choice due to moving toward digital formats. I've had a past coworker who just couldn't do it on paper and chose to use a calendar app instead. She did, however, color-code the subjects the same way lots of people will color-code their personal calendars for different members of the family. It helps keep everything straight. Do what works best for you! It's your sanity after all!

GRADING

Once the students have turned assignments into the in-basket, either I or my TA will take things out of a class slot and directly put the papers into a two-pocket folder that is the same color as the class (look for better quality as you'll use these daily for years). I have about three sets of all six class colors. The two-pocket folders are laminated, causing the pockets to be sealed shut. I just leave them this way and use the folder the same way you'd use a regular file folder. Just slide the items in between the covers. These full folders are then placed directly on my counter to be graded. I don't usually have anything put on my desk by anyone other than myself as it will get lost or mixed in with something else. This two-pocket colored folder system works amazingly well and I *have not lost any assignments* since beginning this process.

As grades are all now mostly computerized, many teachers will input scores directly from the assignment onto the computer and not keep any paper grading sheets. PSA for still printing out paper versions: I have chosen to still use a written grading sheet because there have been times when I've accidentally deleted the wrong student's score, or something similar on the computer, and then I have had no way to find it. Therefore, I print out blank score sheets for each class at the beginning of the term. These are easy to hand over to the TA when grading or take home if I plan to work from there. I also have a customized clipboard especially for just my grade sheets, which makes it faster to locate them anywhere around my desk. I'll do just about anything to make it easier to find something or know exactly what to do with it.

All assignments are graded and recorded on these score sheets. Once I have input their score into the computer, I highlight that particular grade on the score sheet using the color of highlighter that matches the class. This makes it super easy to locate the particular grade a student might be concerned about. Also, by highlighting those that have been input to the computer, it is easy to locate any late assignment scores that still need to be input because they are not yet highlighted.

I print out the grade sheets on ivory, tan, or gray paper instead of white so they are easy to recognize right away. The nice thing about these colors of paper is that the highlighted color will still show up true. I have discussed this process with younger teachers and can see that this might come across as a bit overkill to them, but it really does work! The added step might take a minute longer but is *very* much worth its time in the long run. I've been able to correct several issues by doing it this way. Also, when a student comes to ask about a grade, I can easily show them on the paper and not have to pull it up on the computer if it isn't already. It depends on which one is easier to get to at the moment.

I don't really delve into the way my fellow teachers do this process, but I've had several student teachers and TAs comment on how easy this makes things compared to when they have worked with other teacher's methods of grading. I don't ask any questions; I just take them at their word and say thanks. The rest of the students really appreciate it too.

I don't like to return most assignments to the students, especially quizzes and tests . . . and now even most worksheets. As years have gone by, I have observed more and more students who will just copy another student's graded paper without a second thought. For some reason, it doesn't always resonate with them that this would be considered cheating like it does to me. I want all students to do their own work, especially on assignments where it asks for their opinion or feelings about the topic. If I keep their work after grading, then this doesn't happen.

These papers used to just go into a general Do Not Return plastic drawer (you could use a basket or something else that you have access to) so if a student claims that there has been an error in recording the grade, the papers are all easily accessible. I hand them the small drawer and if they can find their assignment, I'll fix the grade. This is why different assignments are printed on different colors of paper. I can then tell them to just look at the blue pages or the pink pages for example. I recycle all of the work about two weeks into the following semester.

One further step on this topic of not returning assignments is to find smaller baskets or book/binder bins (see Suggested Resources) in your class colors. I just barely started this procedure last year, and it has been super helpful; all of the items not returned go into their individual class's Do Not Return bins. It makes it easier to find *any* papers you're looking for. Some students will ask for a specific item if they're interested in keeping it. Sure makes it easier to locate.

SUBSTITUTES

One of the best examples I have for using color-coding and using the class period colored baskets is when I have a sub for the day. I pull out the three baskets for the classes being taught that day, which include a current seating chart that is all ready for the sub to use. I place all items needed for that class in its respective basket. I stack the baskets with the first class being taught on top and place them either on my desk or on the teacher podium.

Inside the top basket is my lesson plan for the entire day. I usually just hand write them on a legal pad and use a highlighter in its matching color over the class period heading of the class being explained. This helps the sub to know which basket is needed for which class and section of the lesson plan.

I've been lucky to have had preferred substitutes over the years who will regularly cover my classes. They've known exactly how I like things done and make it super easy for me to write up my plans. They will fill in the attendance sheets while in class so I can come back to having it all taken care of. Here is what one of them had to say about covering my classes:

"It's a substitute's dream to walk into a classroom like Jana Pendleton's. Lesson plans and learning activities are guaranteed to go smoothly because of her organization and attention to detail. Everything from lesson plans to scissors are color-coded. Each group of students not only works efficiently, but cleaning up is almost like magic. It just happens and is amazingly effective. Her color system is so easy for students and definitely adds to their success in completing assignments. It's easy to see why students love her classes." —Linda A. Stokes, thirty-year FCS Teacher

Linda has since retired from subbing. My current preferred sub, Amanda McKay, has mentioned several times how much she loves the seating charts in particular, as well as having the colored baskets. Because she is a great teacher in her own right, she loves this system and has expressed that it allows her to actually teach my classes because she has everything she needs in one place. Last year she covered my classes for an entire month. It went so smoothly due to these things and more of what is coming up in the following chapters.

PART 2

In-Depth Organization

Part 2 is full of ideas on how to go deeper into the details of it all. These are great suggestions that you can implement just one at a time and in any order you choose. Yay! These ideas include much more than the color-coding we've just discussed; you'll learn tried and true ways to actually organize all of the essentials you need to do your job well. All of the "stuff" you don't necessarily learn about in college.

Much of this will build upon the previous information learned, but it is entirely different in how it is used. This will include those items that you might wish you had had on hand your first year of teaching. Then you actually acquire some, or a lot, of it your second year, but you're not exactly sure where it is located when you need it, or where to put it after you've used it. I purposefully put all of this great information in a separate section so it would not become overwhelming. Once you feel ready to dig in deeper, go for it!

CHAPTER 5

Teaching Materials

Once you've mastered the tips given in Chapter 1, start implementing the tips in this chapter, which build upon the strategies you've already learned about teaching materials.

THREE-RING BINDERS

I've always taught with a three-ring binder full of anything that possibly pertained to what I was teaching. I used to find the largest ones I could so that everything was together in one place, but they just became too heavy. I was forever carrying them home for the evening, so eventually I broke it down by units.

Most units will fit into half- or one-inch binders. These are fairly inexpensive and are often available at secondhand and wholesale stores. I really like the white ones with a clear-view cover so I can make a cover page and a spine label out of colored cardstock that matches the class subject.

Just a PSA about using three-ring binders to teach from: Several years ago I had to stop working for an entire semester with only one day's notice (saving the telling of that story for another day)! The young woman who took over my classes for me had only just completed her student teaching experience. Here is what she had to say about it:

"Part of me was thinking 'how could I possibly teach five preps with so little experience?' Then it happened, Jana started opening cupboards and filing cabinets full of corresponding color-coded binders full of straight-forward lesson plans and in-depth background info, worksheets, hands-on learning activities, project examples, exams, and answer keys. She took me to her computer and showed me all of the corresponding PowerPoints and video clips. Everything I could possibly need to successfully teach her classes was all bundled up together in one easy-to-use package. Looking back, now with more experience, I feel like I did the unbelievable only because Jana's system and organization made it so easy. This system makes teaching the joy it should be for both teacher and student, and produces a higher quality of instruction and learning at a lower cost of overall time spent in preparation. Once set up, everything in this system works together to create minimal time waste and quality outcomes." —Amelia Gudjenov, former colleague

Of course there needs to be a spot to store these binders. If you're lucky, there will be a cupboard where they can "hide" or a shelf where they can "rest." I've used either or both depending on which school I was teaching in. My cupboard doors now have a matching label to its counterpart on the corresponding file drawer. Now I don't even have to think about where to look or where to return the binder.

Making complete packets for an entire unit used to scare me to death. I never knew exactly what to put in them or in what order. It takes time. You need to teach the same subject over and over again to get to know how it will work best for you. I used to be 100% intimidated by the other teachers who were always so prepared. It honestly took me years to be able to do this. Hopefully it will only take you a term or two.

Once you feel like you're ready, make packets with a colored sheet for the cover and white paper for the pages. We are fortunate to have a copy center in our library who will make these for us. When I just had the unit packets copied individually and handed out one at a time, I always made sure the new copies were the same colors as the older versions of that same unit to match any that were left over so I could use them up.

Just to feed the obsession . . . I can take this a couple of steps further, but it is not necessary for you to do so if you're not so inclined. As I mentioned earlier, I teach out of three-ring binders. I will put a piece of duct tape on the bottom of the spine of the binder which matches the color of its corresponding packet *and* they match the colors of the labels on the hanging file folders too! It cannot get any easier than that! Especially for a long-term sub.

CRATES

On the counter behind my desk I have half-sized file crates made to hold hanging folders. One crate for each subject, or I'll use one for a class that is just being taught the first semester and then flip it around to be used for the subject I teach in its place during the second semester. I use a full-sized sheet of paper (the color of the subject labeled with the name of the subject) in a sheet protector on the front of the crate.

In each crate on the counter I keep one hanging folder for the entire year of the most important documents such as the State Strands & Standards (printed on corresponding colored paper) and use the rest of the space to put all of the hanging folders pulled from the file drawer which pertain to the *current unit I'm teaching* in that particular class. If I have anything that I want to use in teaching this subject sometime in the future, like an idea from a colleague, it will go into that crate. Also, whenever I go to a workshop or conference and get great ideas that I want to use in my classes eventually, I put it in its corresponding crate. Then when I think about something that was presented, I know exactly where to look for the information, and it isn't lost in some notebook or on a random bookshelf. *I don't teach from the crates, and students never touch them.*

There is a cart next to my teacher's podium in front of the classroom that holds a half-size crate similar to these, and it will hold anything I am currently using in my classes for any given unit such as files, binders, books, etc., that are needed just for that day.

As seen in the above illustration, the rectangular class period paper baskets reside on top of the half-crates for each subject. Sometimes there is more than one basket on top if the same subject is being taught in more than one class period. Now remember that the *label on the front of the crate matches the subject* being taught but the *color of the basket on top corresponds to the class period(s)* in which it is being taught. It's easy to remember because the label on the crate also states the name of the subject it is holding.

REQUIRED DOCUMENTS

Something unique to a few of the subjects I often teach is that I not only have to require a signed disclosure document but also a legal guardian permission form from the state. This form is due to the sensitive nature of some of the topics we will discuss. The forms also need to stay on file for one to two years depending. One other item that I like to keep track of for each student is a fee receipt if applicable.

It took a while, but I finally figured out a way to do this easily and always have access to it if needed. I have a one-inch binder for each of the class colors I'm using. I have them clearly labeled as Disclosures, State Forms & Receipts on the front and on the spine. Once the forms start coming in, I have my TA check them off on my printed grade sheet and then place them stapled together in the correct class's color binder in alphabetical order. If students ever question if I'm "sure I didn't just misplace it," I pull out the binder and turn right to the place where their papers need to be. It's all too organized for them to argue! When a new semester begins, I will empty the binder, store the papers that are required, and recycle the rest. New documents from the new term will now refill the binders.

"As I've worked with Jana in her classroom, it amazes me how she has a well-thought-out solution for so many things I had not thought of. When I became a new teacher, I found myself using her tricks to manage my classroom, track grades, and organize various lessons and course materials. Not only are her ideas helpful but they do not require much additional preparation time."
—Kendra Call, former student teacher

CHAPTER 6

Getting Students Organized

Once you've mastered the tips given in Part 1, start implementing the tips in this chapter, which build upon the strategies you've already learned.

WHAT DID WE DO LAST TIME? (WDWDLT?)

Every teacher knows that is the only way students ever seem to phrase that question! It gets old, especially when numerous students are asking it during the same class period. In the back of my classroom I have a full-size crate on the counter with a big bright sign on the front that reads: What Did We Do Last Time?

In the crate I have a hanging file folder for each subject I am currently teaching with a large label attached all the way across the top of the folder with the name of its subject. Of course the label and the folder are in the same color as the files hanging behind it. Once I hand out any new papers to the students, I will place the folder with leftover copies in the crate behind the correct subject label.

When I am asked if they missed anything, I always tell the students to look in the What Did We Do Last Time? crate. They find their class subject and then look behind it. I'll tell them if any of the papers in the files don't look familiar to them, they probably need one. I have them ask their tablemates for directions if needed, as we know anyone who teaches something learns it better themselves. If direction is still needed then I am happily available to help.

Assignments will remain available in the WDWDLT? crate until the end of that unit. I then refile the folders in my filing cabinet and tell the students it is too late for full credit. I'll hand them a copy from my file drawer with a certain percentage off written at the top, or just leave the file in the crate for as long as I am willing to still accept it for full credit. I will allow certain items to be turned in clear up until the end of the term such as a signed disclosure or a "definitely required" assignment. It is important to understand that this WDWDLT? crate, out of all of the different crates, drawers, and files I have mentioned in this book, is the *only* one that the students interact with themselves.

One thing that annoys us teachers more than just about anything is when a student takes the last copy of something out of a file folder. My first few years of teaching I would just attach a sticky note to the front of the original paper stating "ORIGINAL" thinking it would work; however, that never kept the students at bay. The sticky notes always fell off, got attached to another paper, or disappeared altogether. It took a while, but I finally found a remedy for this as I don't plan on checking this crate for copies every single day.

A little known (at least to me) product exists that serves as a sheet protector but does not have the flap on the left with the three holes punched in it. They are sort of the old-fashioned remedy for sheet protectors and do not have a flap on the left side. Holes are punched in them as if there would also be holes punched into the paper inside of it. These are called "full-size sheet protectors" and are readily available on Amazon. Just make sure to carefully read the description. (See Suggested Resources in the back of this book.) I now always keep my original copy in one of these sheet protectors in the hanging file folder.

Students are less likely to ever try to take it out as it looks "official." Usually all of the copies are on colored paper while the original is always white. A less expensive option for the full-size sheet protectors mentioned above is to just use regular sheet protectors and either trim off the flap (to not block the label tab on a manila folder) or just use them as is anyway if in a hanging file folder.

STUDENTS' STUFF

I really like it when students leave their workbooks or notebooks in the classroom. They don't have the excuse that they left them at home, in their car, or other (opposite A or B day) backpack. I have shelves just inside the classroom door that have plenty of space for what is needed. This is when color-coding really helps them.

For example, in my Interior Design class, the students are working on building a portfolio and they store their work in a three-ring binder on one of those shelves. I give them a four-to-five-inch piece of duct tape, which matches their class period's color. They put it on the spine of their binder and then write their name on it with a permanent black marker. I've had up to five different class periods at a time storing their notebooks on those shelves and it's worked well every time.

STUDENT WORKBOOKS

This last year I made workbooks for the Interior Design students similar to the workbooks I have previously made for my Child Development, Adulting, and Financial Literacy students to have all of their packets and important papers in one place. Once I had a system down for a class, I got all of the copies made ahead of time and had my TAs collate them, punch them, and then insert the coil spiral binding. I hand these out within the first few days of class, and the students seem to really like using them. It keeps them organized and current even if they miss a day of class.

TURNING IN UNIT NOTEBOOKS

As stated earlier, in some classes I have students turn in an entire unit's worth of work together. If you have a class where students turn in work the same way, here is an idea I've used and *loved*. In Interior Design, we do "unit notebooks," which are really just a full packet of notes with additional portfolio assignments added.

Once we complete the unit of study, their notebook for that entire unit is due within a week. I have them take their work out of their three-ring binder and place it in a pronged two-pocket folder that I have given them. All portfolio pages are in a sheet protector (front/back) in the exact order listed on the notebook's rubric. All rubrics are printed on paper that matches the color of the unit's packet. The students have a much easier time with me telling them it was part of the pink notebook or orange notebook rather than calling them by their name such as Presentation Methods or the Elements of Design.

These pronged folders are purchased way ahead of time in the summer at Walmart for around twenty-five cents apiece. All of the second period's class folders are orange, sixth period's folders would be blue, etc. Once I've graded and returned them, the students empty out their work and place it back in their three-ring binders. Then the two-pronged notebook is empty and ready for the next unit's work to be turned in when completed. The graded pages in the three-ring binder comprise a final portfolio for the student.

CHAPTER 7

Deep-Dive Organizing

When my middle son, Sage, was just a baby, he was in Primary Children's Medical Center for about a week. While we were there, we experienced a miracle of healing (saving the telling of that story for another day). In addition, we were given several toys, books, blankets, and stuffed animals. One of the greatest gifts came in the form of a wooden block shaped in a half circle and likely cut out of a two-by-six piece of lumber. It was painted like a rainbow and had ten holes drilled in the wide, flat side of it. In each of these holes was glued a Crayola coloring marker's lid with the marker stuck inside. It was just such a simple idea but created a way for the markers not to get lost or left without the lid on!

I'm not sure why, but it took quite a few years until I realized that I could recreate several of these for use in my own classroom. The result has been amazing!

Students love to use them, and when a marker runs dry, I just replace it by inserting the new marker into the original lid!

Each table gets their own wooden block to use.

Classroom packs of Crayola markers come with sixteen different colors. My husband used a two-by-six piece of lumber and cut it into rectangular pieces about nine inches long and drilled the sixteen holes into it. I had the wood shop at the school run them through the planer to make them nice and smooth. I painted the blocks with an enamel-type paint and hot-glued the lids into the holes. People are always impressed and ask where I got the idea. Much thanks to the kind volunteer who made this for the hospital, who ultimately gave it to us!

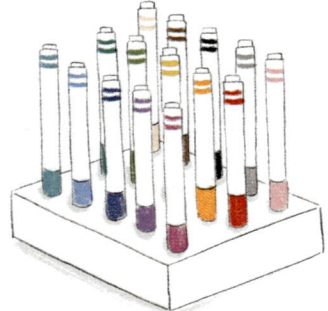

COLOR-CODING TABLES & SUPPLIES

I teach with tables in my room rather than individual desks. Six tables with six students sitting at each table. I have the tables not only numbered one to six, I also have them—you guessed it—color-coded in the colors of the rainbow. I print out some numbers in a fun font on colored paper for the labels. Table number one is red, and it continues through to a purple table number six.

Workbooks

In some of my classes I provide a workbook in place of requiring students to bring a three-ring binder to leave in the classroom. In order to store these books on the same shelves, I have found that durable book and binder holders work well (see Suggested Resources). I have students put their workbooks into the bin that matches their table color—no need for labels. Someone from each table will pick up the entire bin and take it to their table at the beginning of class. Then when the bell rings, they will return their workbooks to the bin on their table and then place it on the shelf on their way out the door.

Supplies

Table color-coding is also helpful for keeping track of all of the supplies required for teachers to have on hand no matter what the age or subject it is that they teach. In the back of my classroom I have a two-by-four and a four-by-four Kallax shelving unit from IKEA and have purchased sets of plastic drawers that are also labeled one to six with the corresponding color of duct tape behind the numbered label.

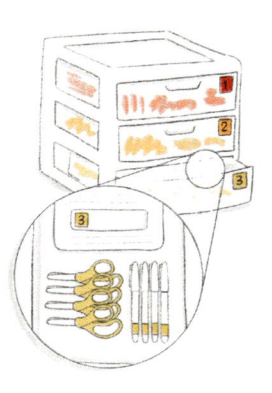

Now this next part is not a requirement, but hey, if you haven't yet figured out that I'm a bit obsessive, then it won't surprise you. Not only do the items in the drawer have a small piece of duct tape on them so they'll be returned to the exact same drawer, I've searched and found some supplies in the correct color. For example, all scissors and rulers match the color of the table. Bottles of rubber cement and black permanent markers have the matching duct tape wrapped around them.

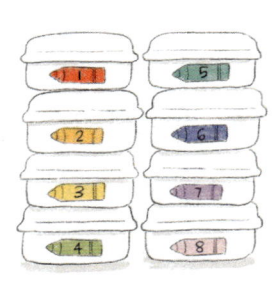

Pencil boxes make a great way to store items like crayons and colored pencils. I have created labels and printed them on the six colors of paper to keep them separate. I often find colored pencils and crayons on the floor after class, and this way I know into which box they need to be returned. It keeps a full set of colors for each table. I don't always have them use their matching box, I just hope they get the suggestion of it most of the time.

Scrap Paper

Scrap paper leftover from projects has always made a huge confusing mess. Students can't locate what they want so they start with another new piece of paper. This just creates more scraps. As a solution for this mess,

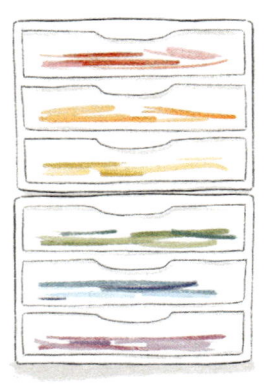

I have sets of clear twelve-by-twelve drawers labeled with the different colors. One drawer is for black, gray, and white, another for brown, tan, and beige, and then one each for the other six main colors. It keeps all the paper organized and easily accessible for the students' use.

Unit-Specific Sets of Supplies

Amazon carries some half-sized pencil boxes which I use for smaller class items. For example, in our color unit, they color a small color wheel using only red, yellow, and blue colored pencils. I have six sets of just these three colors stored in six of the half-sized boxes—one for each table. I also have other assignments where they use specific sets of something like dice or cards and have found that I can use these half-sized boxes super easily. I have about five different sets designated for specific days, and I store all of them in one of the paper boxes in my work closet. More on storage later in this chapter.

Magazines

Magazines are necessary for students to locate pictures for different creative assignments. For many years I used inexpensive dish pans I purchased at Walmart. After a while though, they would start to crack and break due to the weight of the magazines. Magazines are difficult to store and maintain, but I've since found a solution for these as well. A company I love called Really Good Things (see Suggested Resources) sells divided picture book bins. I use these and yes, there are six boxes colored from red to purple. For these though, I have the students choose the bins randomly so they can have new and different magazines each class period.

However, at the end of the semester, each table cleans and organizes their "correct" bin and supply drawer, which matches their table's color. I also have each table clean out the drawer of scrap paper that matches the color of their table as well. This gives some accountability for their cleaning assignments.

Games

When I create a new game for any class that requires a set of cards for them to use, I print one set on red, a set on orange, one on yellow, etc. Sometimes I'll use the pastel version of these colors like pink, peach, canary, mint, baby blue, and lavender.

When playing a memory/concentration type game, I go ahead and print them out on the six colors and laminate them. When I set up the game, I will match them as follows: the terms on red cards with the green cards having only the definitions, then I use the red definitions with the green terms for a different table. I follow those using blue with the orange, and the purple with the yellow. This way the students are only choosing one from half of the deck and the other card from the other half of the deck. It keeps the game from lasting too long and makes it a simpler game for them to play.

For playing BINGO, I have six recycled chewing gum containers full of beans/buttons with a piece of colored duct tape on the container for each table. I've collected all of this over the years so don't expect to have them all at once.

STORAGE

Just to add a bit of perspective here, I have taught at four different high schools and had a couple of different classrooms in one of them. I've had rooms with nice huge storage closets and rooms without. I've taught with students at desks and with students at tables. Sometimes those tables were round so some students sat with their backs to me, and during the pandemic, every student had to sit facing forward by law. I've taught in a designated traditional classroom-type room and taught classes such as Tourism, Fashion, Adulting, and Dating & Marriage in a Food's Kitchen. I've taught in a school over fifty years old and also in a brand-new school. I can tell you one thing: none of them were the same, none of them had the same amount of storage space, and none of them were better than the other. They all have had perks, and they all have had their downfalls. That is the true continuity of teaching: change! And with that change comes flexibility and adaptability. You can have the job of a lifetime and that could change in a heartbeat. I've been there . . . more than once! Sometimes by choice and sometimes not.

One of my teaching assignments had a classroom where the storage items in it began to overwhelm the room itself. Rolling carts of cupboards and shelving units, bins stacked on each other in the corners, makeshift tables to hold important items, and absolutely no room for anything else. I barely had room for student tables . . . let alone chairs around them full of teenagers! The school itself had grown to capacity in the number of students in its boundaries, and it was time for a new high school to be built. Our school was going to dramatically change in number as about one-third to one-half of the students would be moving to the new high school. What that also meant was there were going to be less teachers needed there as well.

One day an architect came into my classroom and asked me what I really liked about my room and what I would change about it if I was able to design it from the beginning. I named two items: I'd love a sink for painting and cleanup as well as a closet for storage. Ever heard the quote attributed to Plato that says, "necessity is the mother of invention"? Well, this is a great example. I had to make my classroom work *for* me instead of *against* me. No matter the situation you find yourself in, there are ways to make things work . . . *and* look good! It's time to get creative and be able to do it on a budget!

Make it easy on yourself by first drawing out the floorplan of your classroom. Use grid-lined paper where one square equals one foot in real life. Also create your storage pieces and cut them out to scale so you can move them around on the floor plan. This will really save your back by not having to manually move the furniture, plus it'll save you tons of time! Find some sort of configuration that will work best for you and your students. Once everything has a place, then it's time to worry about camouflage.

How can you make it look less cluttered and almost like you meant to have it look that way on purpose? Having the storage shelves on wheels actually turned out to be great for me. I filled them up and then turned them around so that when you were looking at them, you only saw the back side (this works if the back of the cart is finished). I could pull them out easily enough if I needed something stored on the shelves. This solution is great when you put your less-often-needed items there.

Put like-things together. Line up the filing cabinets, put all the tall supplies such as poster board, foam core, and matboard standing up in the same corner, stack boxes or plastic storage containers underneath tables or up high on cupboards. Try to use the same size and shape of containers and pay attention to *how* you label them (see my solution below). Keep it simple and professional.

When our new school was being built, I applied for the job opening as the department chair in their FCS department. I got the job in November of the school year prior to the opening of the new school. It was now my job to order every item that would be needed for our classrooms, the culinary kitchen, foods room, child care center, preschool, sewing lab, and interior design lab. It was a daunting task at best and completely overwhelming. Yes, of course I used color-coding for keeping track of orders and such; I just assigned colors to the specific subject areas. No matter the task at hand, I can always find a use for color—even if it's just using a highlighter on the edges of white paper so I can find those orders by category more quickly.

When I was finally allowed into the new school just a few weeks before school was to start, I went to the interior design room and found not only a sink but an amazingly large closet as well! I knew it wouldn't take long to fill it! Starting out with so much empty space was almost as intimidating as feeling like I didn't have enough space. I started by putting like-things together, and as the amount of items grew, I got the empty paper boxes from the copy center in the library and began to label them with a full sheet of paper made into a sign to cover the entire end of the box. Of course it was printed onto a piece of paper in the correct color for the subject it was to be used in.

I would label the box with the name of the entire unit or just the name of the specific activity if it had enough items to fill an entire box. As an example, I have a box devoted to just Elements of Design but then another box is labeled for just one activity within that unit such as the Cookie Color Wheel. It is in one of these paper boxes that I store all of my half-sized pencil boxes with the different colors of crayons or colored pencils and the special sets of dice and cards.

This is the second classroom I've had that has

a large closet. If you are lucky enough to have a decent-sized closet in your room, here is an idea you may not have thought of. I have propped open the door and placed my desk in front of the open door. It is a way to claim that area as my territory—not for the students. When I first did this, my boss just shook his head and thought I must be crazy . . . that was over a dozen years ago. It turned out to be another genius idea that came about almost by accident.

I must say that I love my closet-turned-workroom. By having my desk set up in front of one of the closet doors and keeping all of my file cabinets just inside the closet door, this makes all of that area an extension of my classroom. Sort of like having a personal office attached to my room behind my desk. I am constantly going in and out of it. My student teachers and TAs use it as their mini office, and the counter in there helps me keep all of my curriculum organized with the crates mentioned in Chapter 5. I also have a desktop computer and a scanner/printer available to use as needed stored in there . . . even a mini-fridge and a microwave too!

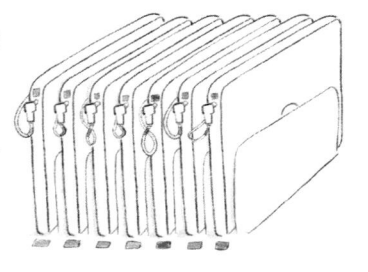

I am fortunate to be able to have a cart full of forty Chromebooks in my classroom. I have always hated using the community carts due to items being left unplugged so they were dead or cords that seemed to never reach the notebook they were meant for. I found a solution using my colored electrical tape. It took two of us four hours to complete, but it was worth every minute and kept everything in working order. It was easy for me to check at the end of each class period and know exactly what needed to be plugged in where.

RANDOMIZING STUDENT NAMES

My oldest daughter, Kylee, also got her teaching degree in family and consumer sciences education. When she was doing her student teaching, she came up with an idea that I think is genius, and of course I use it myself now.

Oftentimes teachers will use some way to call on students randomly. One common method is using popsicle sticks. I've seen this a lot in elementary schools, and it is still highly encouraged by our district to use them in high school as well. Administration will usually bring it up when doing evaluations if a teacher is not calling on enough different students. Kylee created some of these using jumbo popsicle sticks. Her awesome idea was to paint about a third of the stick all the way around using different colors of acrylic paint, one for each of her class periods to keep them straight (why didn't I think of that?).

Instead of writing directly on the stick itself, she applied narrow masking tape to the unpainted end of the stick and then wrote the students' names on the tape. This way the sticks can be used over and over again! She started with the painted ends up and then as students were asked questions, she put their stick back in upside down until it was time to start over.

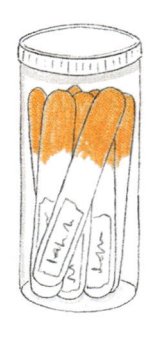

I now have six sets of these jumbo popsicle sticks painted with acrylic paint in each color of the rainbow. I made forty of each and have found that they fit really well, by class, in a recycled Crystal Light container. At the end of the semester I just tear off the masking tape and reuse the popsicle sticks. Like I said, genius!

SUPPORTING MATERIALS

In Child Development, I would usually like to start class each day by reading a children's book to them. Some teachers have their students sign up and bring a book from home or the library to read. Just in case they forgot or were absent, I liked to have books available. To me it is always better to just have books that fit the topics around what we were discussing in the unit. Therefore, over many years I have collected over fifty books from home or second hand stores to include in my collection.

So here we go . . . in order to remember which children's books fit into which categories or units, I put a colored label for each unit on the edge of the shelf in the cupboard where I store the books. Remember, this label corresponds with the color of the unit's packet. Then on the spine of each book, I also put the same-colored tape. When color-coding things with tape, I always put packing tape over the top—sort of as a type of lamination. I swear this is when the inner librarian in me has come out!

I know it's not like you all teach Child Development and have books to catalog, but it might be possible that you have something else you need to keep track of according to your units of study. Rather than just placing it in a box on a top shelf, maybe you'll be more likely to use it if it's right in front of you and even marked with the unit in which you were planning to use it. Colored tape is always my first go-to item for labeling.

I want to share with you one of the most unique ways/places I've used color-coding. I teach human reproduction in Child Development. The students are supposed to understand the male and female body parts, locate them on a diagram, and understand each body part's purpose.

The students all have black line drawings of the reproductive parts for both the males and the females. I have them color the pertinent parts in specific colors so their pages all match one another. One main goal is that I want them to understand how similar we all are to one another rather than different. There are certain parts that start out exactly the same in both sexes during prenatal development. For example, I have them color the ovaries and testicles red, the fimbriae and epididymis purple, the fallopian tubes and vas deferens tubes blue, the uterus and the prostate orange, etc. It helps them remember the body parts and be able to identify them on an exam later.

I have also used the same method about the fetus in utero. They color the placenta red, the amniotic sac brown, the amniotic fluid yellow, etc. It may seem very strange at first, but it definitely works! The key is that all students' pages are the same colors in the same places because it will help them remember it better. You can refer to that place, item, or body part as having been yellow or orange. We play BINGO as a review for this section where they create their own BINGO cards from a list of the vocabulary words. When I am giving the definition of a particular body part, I will hold up the drawing they all have but with just the one item colored in its assigned color from when we all learned them. I will mount this drawing on that particular color of paper as well. The students will remember them by name, but the colors really help. Many of them say the quiz was "super easy" or "not so bad" thanks to the colors.

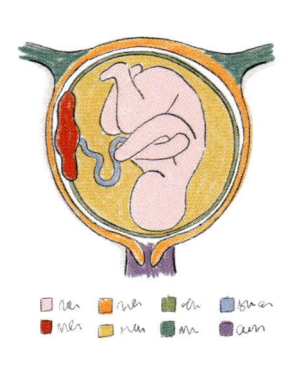

For other subjects, such as geography, all students could color each country, state, or region the same color as given in the teacher's example. Then when reviewing for a quiz or test, have them picture it in their mind and remind them what color it was. I'll bet more students will remember which one is which on a test or quiz than if not color-coded. I've seen this work for parts of a sewing machine, nutrients, the periodic table, parts of a cell, the solar system, and more.

PART 3

Why This Works

When I was in college taking a nutrition class, we were supposed to take notes on all of the vitamins and minerals. I remember that I found it difficult to remember all of the information for the exam, especially on all of the B vitamins; I kept getting them all mixed up. I decided to take the notes for each of the vitamins in a different color of pen.

As I studied for the exam, I would just read through my notes and then close my eyes and try to picture the notes in my mind. I realized after studying for a while that if I could remember what color of ink it was written in, which side of the page it was written on, or whether it was on the top or middle or bottom of the page, when it came time to take the test, I only had to picture the information in my mind. I knew if it was in red ink on the top left it was vitamin B6, and if it was in green ink on the bottom right it was vitamin B12, etc. I was able to do a good job on that exam and keep all of those crazy vitamins in order. It was a game changer for me for sure.

When I am teaching my concurrent enrollment (college level) courses, I always tell them that story about the vitamins and color-coding my notes. I love seeing them start taking notes in colors! It was especially gratifying when a student who graduated a couple of years ago sent me a note telling me how grateful she was for how much I'd taught her about color-coding her notes and keeping track of her important papers. She wrote that she felt so much more prepared in her college courses.

CHAPTER 8

Student Buy-In

I have to say there hasn't been even one semester when a student, or ten-plus students, tells me how much they love my organization. They tell me it makes them happy and they love that they know exactly where everything goes as well as where to find it. Usually it will be one of the last students I would expect to say something. Often it prompts them to organize their rooms, their closets, or just about anything. Sometimes I even get to see photos! I can't tell you how many pictures I've seen of their color-coded closets.

It's times like this that I feel really good about what this system offers. I already know it's worth it for my own sake, but when the students are getting something out of it – even outside of school, that makes it brilliant. My teacher's heart feels all warm and fuzzy. The student I mentioned above is definitely not the only one who has let me know how much they love what they're learning as a *byproduct* of taking my class. It's not like I say, "All right, class, today I am going to teach you how to color-code your sock drawer!" (But don't laugh, it *could* happen!)

I also know I am not the first and only teacher to have ever thought of this. Otherwise, all of these amazing tools wouldn't come in all of these amazing colors. I remember when my daughter was in middle school and her math teacher told her that she needed a two-pocket folder specifically for math only. Oh, yeah, and it *had* to be yellow. I asked her why and she said that the teacher told them that math was always yellow. Mmmkay!?!

The students enjoy being in my room, and that will always help with learning. It is an important but often overlooked aspect of teaching. One that I personally feel is a requirement of teachers. Many students talk about my classroom and how I organize everything. I've become the go-to person for just about everything ranging from tools, a hot glue gun, cardstock, scissors, paper trimmers, etc. You name it! So far, all that I have heard is positive. One girl told me it really was her happy place at school.

Your students will appreciate a happier teacher, a more organized you, a you who is living a more balanced life. They'll tell their friends about taking your classes, and they'll tell their parents what they've learned from you each day. In addition, they'll sing your praises for having taught them not only your content but life lessons as well. You'll be able to give them some tools they can use to be successful in school and in their future, to be able to find what they need, and to know how to keep track of their stuff.

CHAPTER 9

Classroom Environment

One thing that I have found to be ultra-important, and often forgotten, is the environment of my classroom. Students come into my room with their friends, and the friends look around to take it all in. Invariably I am always asked, "What do you teach in here?" They seriously act as if they cannot comprehend that this is a high school classroom and here is why.

A HOMEY FEEL

First of all, my room looks like it belongs in a home rather than at a school. The whiteboard, tables, chairs, and my desk give away the school part. My bulletin boards all have real decorations on them that you would see in a home. I had the dark-red, blaring wall behind the whiteboard painted to a soft shade of blue and the change in temperature was amazing! You honestly could almost touch the change in behavior; it was so real.

I purchase the White Barn Wallflowers Home Fragrance Refills at Bath & Body Works in my favorite subtle scents (Champagne Toast, Vanilla Birch, and Cactus Blossom, just to name a few), and the students comment on them all the time. These come in small liquid inserts where you just screw the bottle into a plastic component that plugs into the wall. The plug-ins come in all colors and styles or just plain if you like. The liquid gets warm and the scent is then distributed around the room. They smell amazing, not at all like the usual room freshener smells. Just the other day I had a student come in and say, "Oh, it's your room!" I replied with a "What are you talking about?" "Oh, I can just smell it from the hall! It's the best! How do you do that?" I just smiled.

Another thing I've done this year that gives it even more of a homey feel is that I have added a table lamp on a timer in the back corner. It turns on at 7 a.m. and off at 3 p.m. It definitely helps students to see their notes during PowerPoints, but I also like the ambient feeling it gives off, even when the overhead fluorescent lights are on. I have it resting on top of two books stacked on top of each other. One of the books is about home decorating and the other is about architecture, both are dated in the mid 1900s. I found them at our local secondhand store, and it just adds a bit of appeal to what's being taught.

STUDENT INSPIRATION

One thing I was encouraged to do several years ago by a friend was to type up some different adjectives of how I would like my room and my students to act or feel. I chose words like engaged, confident, rewarding, helpful, bright, fun, worthwhile, peaceful, willing, mindful, happy, friendly, trusting, welcoming, respectful, pleasant, kind, enjoyable, agreeable, interested, protected, comfortable, memorable, and cooperative.

I printed the words out in a large font on some soft cool colors (about 48 pt. font) and hung them around my classroom. Students have never once commented on them or asked me what they were for. But they obviously see them and read them without really thinking about it. I just know it has made a positive and welcome difference in their attitudes and mine also.

At first I hung them up all around the room . . . all of them at the same time. Now I only have a few on the closet door behind my desk. I change them out every so often, and if a day comes when I want a lot of participation and activity, I change the words—compared to those days when I need them to be calmer and more willing to listen. Whether you believe in it or not, it's an idea to try even if you're just a little bit intrigued.

In addition to the door behind my desk, there is a second door which leads into that amazing "Mary Poppins" closet. Above this second door it reads, "Graduation Countdown." Imagine one of those calendars used in preschool through second or third grade. They have squares with the date numbers written on them over a background that represents the month. For example, January might be a snowman or a snowflake, February most likely will be a heart, and so on. I purchased a set of those for August through May and laminated them all.

Beginning at the *top left* corner of the door, I have taped up the date of graduation and then the next square is the school day before graduation and so on (in the reverse order of a regular calendar). It counts the year down *backward* using only the actual dates we have school. There are about fifteen dates that fit across the door on each row. It ends with the first day of school in August just above the height of the door handle.

Every day after school I take off the current date which begins at the *bottom* of the numbers. Slowly the numbers just disappear their way to the top of the door. It's my way of counting down the school year, but it's also a conversation starter and reminds those seniors that they're getting close to the end.

This year I added a space for fall and spring break as well as when the semester will change. Once the students actually figure out what it is, they think it is quite cool and comment on it as the bottom moves its way up the door similar to shortening a paper daisy chain. I originally used to make one of those and cut off a link each day. That evolved into what you see in the illustration today.

MAKING IT YOUR OWN

On my back wall I have cupboards. The top of the cupboards is my favorite area to decorate in my classroom . . . remember I teach Interior Design. I do think your classroom should in some way reflect your personality and, if possible, the subjects you teach. So back to those cupboards. I have always put items up there that help to teach my subjects or remind students of things I've taught them such as architectural features for example. Over the years I've noticed that they aren't even paying attention to what is up there, even if they can see examples of items that are on their quiz!

So this year, I decided to do something different. I decorated this space just for me! I love beaches, Paris, and all things Disney. Now that is quite a combination. On the right I have a simple arrangement of a few items that represent Paris. On the left I have a "Hello" and my latest word of the year, "Joy." But it's the middle that really counts. It's an assortment of beachy items with glass jars of sand from different beaches I've visited. I look up at this arrangement every single day, sometimes all day long. And I think it's pretty fantastic. It makes me love my room too!

CHAPTER 10

Advice And Lessons Learned

1. Just START—no matter where you are at the time.
2. New teacher or a seasoned teacher, doesn't matter—there's something for everyone!
3. Beginning of the year or middle of the semester, doesn't matter.
4. Do it right the first time—then you won't have to do it over.
5. It's a process. There's *always* room to improve.
6. If everything has a place, then everything can be in its place, and it will be easier to keep up.
7. It may seem overwhelming at first. Just start with one thing and add as you go when you feel ready to do so.
8. The best part of this system is that you won't have to think about it, take time to read it, have to figure it out, etc.

9. "No pencil on final versions of *anything*, unless you can call it art or math." —Jana
10. I don't profess to know everything.

There are a ton of things that I could do in a better/easier/faster/more up-to-date way than I do. I will admit that I have become a creature of habit over some things, but they work for me so why change them? As I stated in the beginning of this book, do what works for you and don't worry about the things that don't. Take these ideas and update them in whatever way works for you.

Be flexible. Be willing to change things up. Keep adding new and different things as you go. It is much easier to change and do things differently when it is what you *want* to do, not something out of necessity or because someone tells you that you *have* to do it. Keep looking for updates to the way you do things, but remember, newer doesn't always mean better. Sometimes you need to be willing *not* to change to the newest thing.

Years ago I found myself in a place where I had to come up with ways to cope and change the way I'd done everything in the past. It's been quite the journey, but I'm not complaining. I'm grateful to my mom who gave me the skills I needed to handle my new normal. Without them I would still feel like all I did was run around in circles.

I still forget a lot of things—just ask the people I work with and live with. Do I make it to every meeting? No. Do I remember everything that needs to be done?

No. Is there a good reason? Yes. Do people understand or need to know why? Not necessarily.

Right now teacher burnout is a real thing. Teachers are leaving the profession in record numbers! But our kids need good teachers! There are tons of articles, podcasts, workshops, social media posts, and professional development offerings for teachers' well-being. I can identify with the characteristics of burnout, of feeling unappreciated, unfulfilled, and stressed out. But I think it's more a sign of the times. The years of going through the COVID pandemic as a teacher have really taken its toll.

So many teachers are out there who desperately need a solution. Teaching as a long-term career is becoming less common due to early burnout. One way to combat that overworked, underpaid, overwhelmed, unorganized, fly-by-the-seat-of-your-pants feeling is to get your crap together.

Only you know where it is most needed for you. What part of the job overwhelms you the most? Is it the students' behavior, the administration's requirements, the parental expectations, your *own* expectations, or just the job in general?

Unfortunately I can't change any of that for you, but I *can* help you with organizing the tools of the trade. This will allow you to find the extra time you need to do the things that fill you up and build you up—the things that matter the most!

We all have a coping threshold, and even a breaking point. It may happen at different times and for different reasons for each of us. Most importantly we need to *remember our why.* Why did we choose to become a teacher in the first place? What was it that we wanted to accomplish as a teacher? Who set a great example for us? Was it a teacher you once had yourself who changed your life or way of thinking? Was it possibly a family member who was a teacher and who set a great example for you? For me it was my grandma and her two daughters, my aunts, JoAnn and Jerry.

Why are we feeling so overwhelmed and undervalued? It's true, the pandemic of 2020 did a number on all of us. However, those of us who are "in the trenches" need to go back to our why. It may be time to make some changes in what we're doing, or possibly the way we're doing it, in order to make things happen for us. One great question to ask yourself is "And how's that workin' for ya?" It's so simple to ask, but the answer can change everything. If something isn't working, it needs to be tweaked or changed out altogether.

I heard this quote from Chandler Bolt at a Self Publishing School workshop as I began writing this book: "Change will come when the pain of staying the same becomes worse than the pain of doing the new thing."[2]

This totally speaks to me. It is why people wait until they hit rock bottom before they make a needed change in their lives. Whether it has to do with work, home, or our personal lives, sometimes it's just easier to stay where we are. At least we know *where* we are. It's our comfort zone—even when it's uncomfortable.

---

[2] *Chandler Bolt, Self Publishing School live workshop, June 3, 2022.*

The genius of using color to straighten out our lives is that it is a visible and instinctive process. In fact, if we go back to the definition of color itself "a visual perception that enables one to differentiate otherwise identical objects."[3] It makes perfect sense, it takes no thought to tell the difference between two or more similar items. It takes no time after the original investment of time in setting up your system. And then you'll receive a payday from that system each and every day.

Just like a monetary investment, what you receive is relative to what you're willing to put into it. The more you add to it, the bigger and better your return on that investment. There will come a point when you aren't feeling so overwhelmed. You'll be able to look at what you've accomplished, visually take it all in, and feel good about yourself and what you've been able to do! "Success means different things to different people at different times in their careers, but the key thing about it is that it's a concept that comes from within, *not* from without."[4]

I love my job of teaching young people to become better, more competent, successful adults. I love teaching high school, being around teenagers, and having them look to me for advice and understanding. I love knowing that I can make a difference in the life of a young adult and possibly even their family. This is why I stay.

---

[3] *"Color," Merriam-Webster's Collegiate Dictionary, 10th ed. (Springfield, MA: Merriam Webster: 1998): 226.*

[4] *Geoff Palmer, How To Write a Book: 12 Simple Steps to Becoming an Author (New York, NY: PodSnap Publishing Ltd, 2019): 119.*

As I said in the beginning, I've always wanted to write a book. For many of those years I wasn't sure that it would even be possible. I didn't know where to start until I was given some guidance and specific steps to follow. That is what I hope to have done for you here. I can't promise you it will fix everything, but it definitely won't hurt.

Remember *your why*. Why did you search for this book? Why did you purchase it? What were you looking for? Maybe it was a gift or something you found completely by chance. I don't believe in coincidences. One of my favorite words in this world is serendipity. Interestingly enough, Merriam Webster's dictionary defines it as "the phenomenon of finding valuable or agreeable things not sought for." Now that you know what you know, it's time to take action! Every change begins with one tiny step...the time is now. Do *something;* every step you take will get you closer to where you want to be. Mmmkay!?! Consider this to be your personal invitation to get going . . . make a difference in your own life, and in the lives of your students!

Suggested Resources

MY FAVORITE RESOURCES

Here is a list of some of my favorite places to shop for organizing items . . . especially the items that I've mentioned in this book. Some are online while others (or something similar) are located in most areas of the United States. The bulleted list underneath each resource is a list of the particular items found at each resource discussed within the text. This is not an exhaustive list of all my materials, but it is a really good place to start.

ReallyGoodStuff.com (seen below as **RGS)

- Classroom paper baskets (a must-have)—Chapter 3
- Picture book bins (for magazines and children's books)—Chapter 7
- Book and binder holders with stabilizer wings (for workbooks and my Do Not Return containers—Chapters 1 and 6

Amazon.com

- Various office supplies (delivery to your door is the *best*!)
- Colored hanging file folders
- Full-size sheet protectors (for original documents)—Chapter 6
- Organizational Supplies
- Plastic clipboards (class period colors for seating charts, other colors for anything else)—Chapter 3

Walmart.com

- Pencil boxes, full- and half-size—Chapter 7
- Crates, full- and half-size—Chapter 5
- Two-pocket folders (for grading)—Chapter 4
- Pronged two-pocket folders (for turning in units of work)—Chapter 6

IKEA

- Kallax Cubed Shelving Units
- Containers that fit within the Kallax cubes

Bed, Bath & Beyond

- Wire Cube Organization System (to create inboxes)—Chapter 2

TeachersPayTeachers.com

- Teaching strategies and lesson planning ideas

Teacher Facebook Groups

- Teaching strategies, lesson plans, and ideas

Pinterest Ideas

- Teaching strategies, lesson plans, and project ideas

Dollar Store

- Inexpensive office supplies
- Foam core boards
- Baskets and bins
- Colored folders
- Sketch Pads for planning book pages

MY MUST-HAVES

This list is composed of items I consider to be necessary tools and use on a daily basis. I have several sets of all of these. I even buy my own set to have at home.

- Colored duct tape, colored electrical tape
- Packing tape, regular and extra-wide (gun and dispenser)
- I call it cheap lamination: cover everything to make it more durable.
- Clear transparent Contact paper (not matte)
- White artist's tape (super sticky and easily removable)
- Colored masking tape and dispenser, narrow plain masking tape

- Double-sided tape and dispenser
- Colored electrical tape
- Brightly colored sticky notes (black too!), colored paper clips (easy to find, color-coordinate with subjects or class periods)
- Hanging file folders in all necessary colors (by subject once you can afford it)
- Two-pocket folders (pronged and non-pronged)
- Laminate non-pronged and use for grading.
- Page protectors (for binders) and full sheet protectors (for originals)
- Highlighters, colored ink pen sets, metallic pens and markers
- Crayola colored pencils classpacks
- Crayola marker classpacks, wood block (with holes drilled in)
- Wite-Out tape, colored binder clips
- Paper baskets (14.25"W x 10"D x 3.25"H) (for class periods) **RGS
- Picture book bins (13.5"W x 13.5" D x 7.75"H) (for magazines or books) **RGS
- Durable book and binder holders (for Do Not Return bins or workbooks) **RGS
- Wire cube storage organizers, colored pipe cleaners (for inboxes)
- Half-size and full-size pencil boxes
- Sharpies black (fine and ultra-fine point) and multiple colors including metallics
- Planning book, a copy of mine or someone else's, must have horizontal days of week

- Scanning app on phone (whichever app works best for you)
- This allows you to take a photo of any document, no matter where you are, and include it in your files as a photo or a PDF.
- Wallflowers Scents Home Fragrances from Bath & Body Works

Acknowledgments

I would like to thank my mom, Janice Meikle, for teaching me to do things right the first time, to never give up, to kill them with kindness, and to always care what something looks like. She and my dad, Steve Meikle, built me up with continual love and support. They gave me more than I could possibly ask for while teaching me to strive to always do my best and never settle for less.

Thanks to my husband, Boyd Pendleton, for reminding me what I do right. He has patiently listened to every version of this story. We came together and created our own miracles in spite of everything. His love, encouragement, patience, and support are never ending.

To each member of our family, thanks for being the reason I write. You really are my everything! Kylee, Kevin, Aiden, Dylan, Millie, Jones, and Maizie; Travis and Lindsay; Katelyn, Shay, Kaizley, Brixton, and Wreny; Sage and Flower; and Riley.

Thanks to Chandler, Bella, Michael, Ellaine, Jordyn, Chad, Tyler, and the rest of the group at Self Publishing School. This book would still just be a dream without you and your guidance.

Thanks to Kylee Labrum for designing the cover and drawing all of the illustrations found within the pages of this book. She has an amazing talent; of which not one ounce came from me, her mom.

Thanks to Carly Catt for using her magic to turn my thoughts, ideas, and words into a manuscript that is readable, understandable, and easy-to-follow.

Thanks to my colleagues Glenda, Maribeth, Sue, Lois, Camille, Jen, and Kendra for instigating a unique component in my why for creating this system.

Thanks to Linda and Amanda for coming to my rescue time and time again, even on a moment's notice - and sometimes long-term, to cover my classes.

Many thanks to all of the amazing students, TAs, and student teachers I have been able to enjoy having in my classes. Several of you still stay in touch, and I appreciate your coming back time and again to help me do what needs to be done.

Lastly, to those of you behind the scenes who have been my cheerleaders and best friends, encouraged and supported me always, but especially in this new endeavor in my life: Kami, Tyra, Janel, and Nancy. I love you!

Author Bio

Photo Credit: Michelle Evans

Jana Pendleton has always loved color and organizing since she was a little girl. You can find her straightening and tweaking the small items in stores and spending way too much money in the office supply and crafting aisles while color-coding everything. Jana loves sharing her knowledge with others and having the opportunity to change people's lives for the better.

Her favorite superhero is the one who makes the rest of them look good . . . Edna Mode.

Jana lives in the beautiful state of Utah, is a wife, mother, and gramma. She has an MS in marriage, family, and human development and has taught high school for over twenty years. She hopes this book will help other teachers feel better prepared and more organized and relieve some of their daily stress and worries.

> "Teaching is our gift to the future.
> It is meant to be enjoyed."
> —Jana

> Thank you for
> Reading
> my Book!
> Jana

I really appreciate your taking the time to
let me know how much you have
enjoyed reading my book.

Please take just a moment to leave a helpful review on
Amazon letting me know what
you thought of the book:
colorworksbook.com/review
Thanks so much!

Made in the USA
Coppell, TX
07 April 2023